You Are Not the Only One

You Are Not the Only One

Michell Barker

Editors:
Victoria Troy
Chris Nolan

·

This book is dedicated to women all over the
world who have been sexually, emotionally,
physically, and psychologically abused.
To all the women who have ever
felt abandoned, neglected, depressed, or hurt.
Never allow your past to affect your future.

Alethia,
    Continue to be the light and healer that you are. The world is a better place because you're in it

Michell.

TABLE OF CONTENTS

You Are Not the Only One

INTRODUCTION

Firstly, I want to say thank you for picking up this book and deciding to read it. My name is Michell Barker. You don't know who I am yet, but I am happy our energy has lined up enough for us to connect this way. I have been through a lot of painful and beautiful experiences that I am going to share with you, and I want you to know I am here for you. I wrote this book in the hope that by sharing my personal stories and spiritual principles which have helped me on my journey (along with my rock bottoms), you, too, will be able to relate to them and see you are not the only one who has been through what you have been through. In the beautiful, crushing process of awakening to consciousness, hopefully you will realize you deserve every good thing this world has to offer.

This book has biblical and spiritual principles which have helped me in my journey of healing. Even though I am grateful to my God for His love and sending His son to die for my sins, I am by no means trying to convert anyone to Christianity. I am also not here to judge anyone for anything they have been through. I am here to share my story and my lessons hoping for a domino effect. Maybe then, you will find the courage within yourself to share your story because we really do overcome with the power of our testimony. While you do not have to share your story in a form of a book, perhaps you can share it with your family and friends, or maybe where you volunteer at a school, or at a local shelter. Painful experiences lose their power when we talk about what has happened to us in a safe environment because secrets make us sick. Trauma stays in our bodies and in our minds until we are ready to deal with it. Your trauma will affect every part of your life in a negative way until you decide to acknowledge what has happened to you and talk about it.

If you are Christian, Jewish, Muslim, Buddhist, Sikh, Hindu, Catholic, or practice any other religion peacefully, you are welcome here. If you are agnostic or atheist, you are welcome here. If you are part of the LGBTQIA+ community in any way, you are welcome here. This is a safe space for any and all who want to find their light and want to know they are not the only ones who have suffered in any way. You are welcomed into my vulnerability and to read my story so it may empower some part of your soul, even just to show you that people are perfectly imperfect, and you are exactly who you are supposed to be. Living in Canada, I have had the pleasure of meeting people from all walks of life. I do not believe that because I am a Christian, I have the right to hate anyone. Actually, it is just the opposite: because I am a Christian, I want everyone to feel loved and live well.

I have always found it interesting how entitled people are towards what other people have or feel; how entitled we feel to embarrass, ridicule, or go out of our way to hurt another human being, or even worse: to be completely unresponsive to their needs before having a duty to be empathetic and helpful. But how do we do that for other people when we are berating and punishing ourselves for the mistakes we have made? We do treat people the way we treat ourselves, do we not? This crazy, cruel, and beautiful world needs you to be and grow into who you were born to be and to do on this earth what you were put on Earth to do.

"The only thing necessary for the triumph of evil is for good men to do nothing." - Edmund Burke

Allow yourself to be used by the divine in order to make this world a better place. Pray to God and ask the Universe what you can do to actualize your purpose in this life then be open to the answer given. There are so many exciting things happening in this world you can focus on instead of watching TV all day long and reliving the painful events which have happened to you in the past. You truly are the creator of your life. I would rather make lemonade than live with bad lemons.

You, my dear, are one of the greats, if you allow

yourself to be right where you are. I wish you the best and I am grateful and honoured to be a part of your journey of becoming the best version of yourself!

1. YOUR PERCEPTION IS EVERYTHING

per·cep·tion
(pər-sĕp′shən)
n.
The process of perceiving something with the senses:
Insight or knowledge gained by thinking
An interpretation or impression; an opinion or belief:

What are the stories we tell ourselves repeatedly in our heads? Do these stories reflect your happy memories of the well-deserved vacations you have taken over the years? Are they filled with happy moments with your family growing up? Maybe you remember a time spent in the humid Caribbean enjoying its rich culture, glorious resorts, and delicious food. Or perhaps these memories were from that European trip you took to celebrate a friend's birthday where you experienced its stunning, deep-rooted history inside the famous Louvre in Paris staring at the beautifully small Mona Lisa together. Or just maybe it was the Latin American trip to Mexico where you lay on the hot, sandy, white beach by the salty sea with your friends or family staring in awe at all the vibrant colours in the sunset which fell into slumber before you in all its magnificence. Is it possible the stories you replay in your mind and stick out above the rest are not as nice as those? We all have good and painful experiences inside of us, but it always seems like the painful memories are replayed the most. Perhaps the memory of that heart-wrenching breakup you had with your ex is what you replay in your mind. Your mind is still reeling at the fact that the fairytale ending you were really looking forward to turned out to be your biggest nightmare or a bad bet. Now you stew about all the time and resources you wasted on the person. Did your friends or family members continuously disappoint you growing up? Was there a co-worker who took out their personal frustrations out on you by spreading malicious lies and untrue stories to make your work life miserable and hard to wake up to in the mornings?

So a man thinketh in his heart, so is he - Proverbs 23:7

Everything we do starts with our thoughts. The way we think will determine if we grow, stagnate, or regress because our thoughts create our energy. Our past experiences and how we view them will generate the positive or negative energy which will assist in determining the quality of life you will have in the present. When I was younger, I decided to focus my thoughts on stories which laid a foundation of negative energy for myself and for those around me. I used to feed myself thousands of lies. Stories about how my heart was broken into a million pieces by an ex, how dreadfully neglected I felt in my childhood, or how I believed I should not go after my dreams because, as a single mom, paying the bills took precedence over any aspirations I had for myself. Even though none of those stories were grounded in any actual evidence, I decided to believe it so I could reinforce the negative perception I had about my myself. I would spend countless hours lamenting the decisions I had made when it came to the kind of men I dated or friends I had. A few bad relationships or school experiences did not cancel the friends and family who did care for me, but I certainly interpreted it that way. I convinced myself I was so neglected as a child growing up in Toronto, honestly believing nobody loved me, that I would create and enter dramatic situations which made me feel as though I was living in a telenovela (for those who don't know, a telenovela is a Spanish soap opera which has an extraordinary amount of drama compared to the regular soap operas we watch in North America). I overreacted toward a lot of people because I did not have the right perception of the things which had happened to me. I was not healing the traumatic memories which were so bad my mind had blocked some of them to keep me from imploding.

> *"Life is 10% of what actually happens to you and 90% how you perceive it." - Max Lucado*

Whether your perception of an experience is true or false, positive or negative, it will quickly evolve into your reality and will feel true to you regardless of how the experience actually transpired. You will focus in on the reality you have created from your perception of the experience, and it will become the story you tell yourself. The stories of these painful past experiences I continuously retold myself created a lot of negative energy inside me which turned into self-medication habits, such as drug use and men to name a few. I used these self-destructive habits as an excuse to stifle and suppress my pain and memories; however, they were also suppressing my happiness, skills, and talents which, in turn, prevented me from the ability to step out and pursue my true purpose so I could live a happier life. Your story, as you choose it with your own free will, will justify your attitude and the decisions you make.

The "burden" of our free will is that we can decide what we believe in life. The decisions we make and the people we allow to enter our lives will reinforce some or all those beliefs. A person with low self-esteem will be more likely to allow themselves to be used and manipulated by abusive and narcissistic people. People who value themselves surround themselves with people who treat them well and honour them. People who love themselves decide they are worthy of love and work on being the best versions of themselves. People who work on themselves create the ability to be able to perceive people and experiences they encounter (both past and present) correctly so they can remain in an empowered state instead of a defeated one.

Do you remember the story of Joseph from the book of Genesis in the Bible? Joseph never chose to be sold into slavery. He also never asked to be thrown in jail for doing the right thing, but he did not allow himself to be the victim. When he was sold into slavery, his perception of what happened to him allowed him to run his master's compound. When he was falsely accused of attempted rape and thrown into jail, the perception he had enabled him to run the jail until his time came to become the second most powerful man in all of Egypt. Every injustice placed upon him repositioned him closer to his calling and purpose. What he went through was not by any means easy, but I wonder what his story was going through it... Was he retelling himself the story of his brothers betraying him or being falsely persecuted by a woman who hit on him? No, he retold himself the story of God's plan for his life and the dream God gave him until it came true. I am sure the Pharaoh asked the guards about Joseph before he promoted him. I wonder what would have happened if the guards reported he was just another inmate who was depressed or violent instead of the man who rose to run that same jail the people who put him there wanted him to rot in.

What damages us is not what happens to us, but the story we tell ourselves about what happened to us. Think about this for a moment and come to a moment of awareness with me right now: what has happened has already happened. At this present moment in time, you are fine, and your soul is intact regardless of how you feel. The traumatically painful experience is in your past. Not your present or your future. The only place the pain exists is in your mind. You are keeping the pain alive by repeating the painful version of the story because of the perception you have of what happened to you. If are replaying this story in your mind, you have not extracted the lesson. The experience was there to teach you and you have not healed the piece of yourself that is stuck in that moment. Certain experiences can be left in the past, but some will only go away if you do the work. Suffering, happiness, fear, love, and peace are all produced by the stories you are telling yourself. Every emotional state you experience is rooted in the story you are telling yourself so if you want to change the emotional state, you have to change the story.

John 8:32: Then you shall know the truth,
and the truth shall set you free.

I believe with all my heart that if the truth will set you free, then lies will keep you in bondage. I had to rewrite the story I was telling myself about my past and change my perception of it so I could let it go and move on. I had to dig through all the painful stories which lay waste in my mind and release them by changing the narrative, some of which were admittedly figments of my imagination. I purged from my soul those stories which empowered fear, enabled helplessness, and took me down deeper into the abyss. Part of this process involved speaking with family and friends - maybe an ex or two - with the goal in mind of gaining clarity on past situations whether I liked what they said or not. I created new filters in my mind through reading passages in the bible, reading a lot of self-help books and blog posts, listening to podcasts, watching motivational videos on YouTube, and attending networking events and seminars. I went ham on my self-development journey. All these resources were a major influence on purging the darkness and bringing in the light.

If I felt worthless, I would read scripture which confirmed to me I am a creation of God and His masterpiece. I would meditate on this until I started believing I am, in fact, a masterpiece. I will speak to you about what being a masterpiece is later in the book.

Your past does not define or determine your future, as long as you do not let it. Do not let the way you perceive an experience get in the way of enjoying your life. Being poor as a kid does not determine how wealthy you are going to be as an adult. A major breakup/divorce does not mean you will never meet your soulmate. One or a few bad friends does not mean your best friend is not around the corner. Being abused in any capacity does not mean you are worthless. In fact, if you pick the right story, it can mean rebounding and gaining immeasurable strength to get everything you want.

You can change your story whenever you want. Even though during my childhood and adolescence I felt neglected at the time, I realized later in my life this was not true in the sense I thought it was. My mom was a single mother of three kids working multiple jobs to ensure she could put food on the table, clothes on our backs, and a roof over our heads. My mother had also been through a lot of difficult experiences and was navigating her own trauma and tried her best with what she had. Parenting was never meant for one person and, as a single mom, I had to learn this lesson the hard way. Life may have been depressing as a teenager and I may have lived a toxic lifestyle in my 20s, but I am happy and more peaceful than I have ever been because I changed the way I viewed the things I went through and experienced. Life can still get a little crazy from time to time, but I have the right stories to keep me grounded in love and peace. My prayer is that you, too, may find joy and peace in your heart and the courage to change your story. Joy, happiness, and purpose all come from your heart, your soul, your inner state. You give meaning to your life, not the other way around. You give meaning to your parents, your upbringing, your career, your friends, your schooling, your home, your business, your experiences, your partner, or your pet. If you do not find what you like or what you are grateful for in these situations, you will not enjoy any of it and grow to resent it.

It is your life and the story you tell is what you decide it is. The painful world we live in is the world human beings have created with their free will. You can use your free will, decision-making, and creativity to create a world of beauty and peace by having the right perception of the things which have happened to you and of who you are. If you do that, you will be free to create the world which you have cultivated inside of you for the rest of the planet. How can we love our neighbor if we do not love ourselves? We cannot love people beyond the way we love ourselves or from a place of empty. Trust me I've tried.

2. FEAR

fear
(fîr)
n.
A very unpleasant or disturbing feeling caused
by the presence or imminence of danger
A feeling of disquiet, dread or apprehension

It is fear which stands between you and seeing your dreams and potential realized. Fear is one of strongest emotions which can have profoundly negative effects on how we view our stories. It can completely paralyze us and prevent us from achieving our goals and striving to become our best. To be completely honest with you, I have often let fear stand in the way of my goals and dreams. Fear prevented me from pursuing the things I loved, such as motivational speaking or taking dance lessons because I was afraid of looking bad in front of other people. It was not until I had hit one of my rock bottoms in my marriage that I had an epiphany: I was not going to get out of my situation or make my dreams come true in the absence of fear, so I had to do what I felt was right in the presence of fear to get all the things that I wanted in life.

Everything you want is on the other side of your fear. By facing your fear or fears, only then will you be able to pursue your dreams and ambitions. You will always be put in situations where this emotion will rear its head and there is nothing you can do about it, especially if it is new experience. It has happened many times in the past, and you can guarantee you will find yourself in a situation where this primal emotion will surface again.

FEAR: *False Evidence Appearing Real*

Fear was meant to be a tool to assess the potential danger of a situation, not an emotion that manages your life and talks you out of all the things that you want to do. What it comes down to is how you manage this fear. Think about this emotion as a good crisis management tool instead of the saboteur of your plans. Assess the potential dangers and see if the risk is worth it, but you are never going to not feel fear, especially if you are going after something that you want. I cannot even begin to imagine how many dreams were stopped in their tracks because people decided to hide and chose to opt out of the pursuit of their dreams. How many relationships were ended prematurely or perhaps did not even begin because the overriding thought in your mind was the fear of failure or the fear of being hurt? Fear has no problem taking over your life and crippling you, if you let it.

Just because you fear it, doesn't mean you shouldn't do it

I grew tired of working for multimillion-dollar corporations whose sole focus was their bottom line with a complete disregard for the well-being of their employees. I think of all the time and effort I put into their companies, yet I was never given as much as a thank you for the hard work and years of service I will never get back. I had never felt so unappreciated in my life. I thought maybe it was all in my head and perhaps my perception of the situation was skewed. I decided to move on from the company for which I was working at the time, but before I left, I told the young lady they hired to replace me that the employer had a habit of making his employees feel like they are never doing enough even though you are running the department well. Oddly enough, right after I gave her my opinion this dread came over me and I instantly regretted saying it to her. I told myself the girl I was trying to help did not care about my experience at the company and it was none of my business. I started to feel anxious about the advice I had given her and felt bad I said anything to her at all. When I ran into my replacement a year after I had left the company, she told me she was treated the exact same way I had been. When this particular COO would try to crack down on her she would remember what I said to her, and it made her feel better. Even though she was grateful I had shared my story with her, it was not something I had originally intended to do. This experience taught me a lesson: we can have a fear-based initial reaction to things we do even though we are doing the right thing.

Fear almost prevented me from writing this book. From the moment I decided to write this book, I was drowning in my anxiety the way I almost actually drowned in a community swimming pool when I was eight years old. There was a thick cloud of uneasiness constantly hovering above me for almost the two years it took to write this book and reach my goal. I recall having a conversation with my friend Paul over this very book and expressed the fears I was having. I was being candid with him as I told him I did not think anyone was going to buy or read this book into which I poured my heart and soul. I was worried people would laugh at it and say terrible things about it. This was the untrue story I was telling myself which, if I had let it keep going, would have justified me stopping writing the book. It had no basis in truth, but I was breathing life into it by repeating it and focusing my attention at the negative narrative. Think about it: how am I to know how many people are going to read or like this book? I have never written a book prior to this one, so I do not know what the outcome is going to be. After rambling on about my unrealistic concerns, Paul said something which would end up changing my untrue story. He said, "What if this book talks one person off a ledge? What if it gives a single person hope? Would it have been worth it then?" He was right. If this book does help a single soul, then it would have been worth all the time and effort it took to write it. If it does help just one person struggling with depression, suicidal thoughts, or low self-esteem, it would definitely be worth it. This book has also saved my quality of life just by writing it. It has made me extract my lessons on a deeper level and it has developed me more than anything else I have ever done. Then, one day out of the blue as I was working on my book, the fear I was experiencing subsided. I literally felt the fear leave my being like how I would imagine the red sea parted for the Israelites. I was then able to finish this book at a much faster pace. This book almost did not get written because I am sharing some of my most personal and intimate stories. In the end, I decided to face my fears and write the book I wanted. Now, I am going to let the chips fall where they may. My fear of writing this book subsided while I was in the process of writing it, not before I started. Fear is like a big menacing cloud through which one has to walk in order for it to leave. It will not go away on its own. I am reminded of a quote from a popular children's book which says, "you can't go around it, you can't go under it, you have to go through it." These fear-based stories we tell ourselves are not necessarily based on what is happening in the moment. They are based on what we hope does not happen to us in the future.

I was able to release some of my general fears when I watched a movie called Down to Earth with Will and Jaden Smith (which I highly recommend!). This movie was completely ahead of its time and a lot of people, understandably, did not get the movie. People were disappointed because they went into the movie to be entertained, but this movie makes you think about the very thing people avoid. The movie explained how fear operates, what we should do to overcome it, and the type of people and elements with which we should both surround ourselves and avoid. It explained how fear is created, how to navigate fear, and, ultimately, how to overcome it. The movie completely went over people's heads and made people uncomfortable because people do not want to have the conversation about what they fear. I would say most people walk around having the outward appearance of being fearless, but all of us struggle with some form of fear, especially as it pertains to a traumatic experience which happened to us. You are not the only person who is afraid of the unknown, or afraid of being hurt or embarrassed, afraid of dying, afraid of losing a loved one, afraid of never finding "the one," afraid of getting sick, or never achieving your dreams... the list of fears is infinite and causes people to struggle with them on a daily basis.

"Our deepest fear is not that we are inadequate. Our deepest fear is that we are powerful beyond measure. It is our light, not our darkness that most frightens us. We ask ourselves, 'Who am I to be brilliant, gorgeous, talented, fabulous?' Actually, who are you not to be? You are a child of God. Your playing small does not serve the world. There is nothing enlightened about shrinking so that other people won't feel insecure around you. We are all meant to shine, as children do. We were born to make manifest the glory of God that is within us. It's not just in some of us; it's in everyone. And as we let our own light shine, we unconsciously give other people permission to do the same. As we are liberated from our own fear, our presence

automatically liberates others." - Marianne Williamson

Giving up on your dreams is fear-based and a form of hopelessness. Deep down we all know what we want in life. If we all dig down deep enough, we all have a dream we want to see fulfilled. Some of us are afraid if we step out of the shadows of the people who purposely dim our light to follow our dream, we will lose the role they play in our lives. There are people who have absolutely no issue diming your light if they think it will make theirs shine brighter. They are the ones who are more afraid than you are. If you have to lose people to gain yourself and see your dreams realized, then it is your duty to move on from them. We are all afraid to be our highest selves because maybe we might have to leave people behind who were toxic. In those cases, it might feel as though it's better to have the devils you know than the devils you don't, right? While we should always be cautious and do our research on people, I do find there are also a lot of strangers who are more likely to help you than people you know or family members you have known your whole life. Do not let fear stop you from taking action towards the life you know you want to live. People in your life are either going to get it or they won't, and it is certainly not your job to help them understand who you are becoming. It is, however, your job to become who you were put on this earth to be. By doing that you will move past your fear and discover how wonderful you are and that you don't have to be afraid of yourself, you'll even learn to love your shadows.

3. IT IS NOT GOD'S FAULT

God
n.
(gŏd)
A being conceived as the perfect, omnipotent, omniscient
originator and ruler of the universe, the principal object of
faith and worship
One that is worshiped, idealized, or followed

I went through a long period of my life where I hated God. I blamed Him for all the pain and stress I was experiencing. I could not understand why an all-loving God who professes to love me would allow me to grow up in the circumstances into which I was born, such as not having a father around. I also did not understand why a loving God would allow me to feel so alone and unloved. I blamed him for everything wrong in my life. I remember being so broken one day outside of my apartment building, I just started screaming at God (people must have thought that I was crazy. I just lost it). I grew up in the church, so

I grew up believing God loves you and He was all powerful, so why did He not just change my circumstances and why did I not feel it?

"God has a bigger plan for me than I have for myself."

At the beginning of 2018, I expressed to God I would like to settle all the issues I had with Him which I had built up inside of me for so long. How could I call myself a Christian and not believe God loved me when that sentiment is plastered all over the bible? I believed God loved the whole world, but I could not personalize it to myself. The way I looked at it was I did not have any issue with Jesus or the Holy Spirit; I just could not connect with God the Father as He had been portrayed to me. To help my journey of healing our relationship, the Lord showed me a verse in Job which reads, "Will you really annul My judgment and set it aside as void? Will you condemn Me [your God] that you may [appear to] be righteous and justified?" Was I blaming God in order to dodge responsibility? Is this how I was justifying the bad choices I was making? Was I blaming God for my parents not coming to my basketball games? Did I blame Him for the choice I made in men or friends? Was it His fault I made the decision to get married at the age of nineteen or to hook up with another guy before the ink on my divorce papers was even dry? The blame sounded like this: God, why would you let me marry these men? Why did you give me the parents you gave me? Why are you allowing me to feel all this pain? You don't love me because, if you did, none of this would have happened. I mean, what kind of father figure are you? A good parent would rescue their child and would not allow them to go through these things... the rant was absolutely endless, I blamed him for everything that was wrong in my life. When I look back, I can confidently say I blamed God for the mess I was in because I did not take responsibility for my own decisions and actions. I was not intentionally doing this. At that point, I truly did not know what taking responsibility meant, nor that nothing was going to change until it did.

One of the major issues at play was I was asking the wrong questions. I kept asking myself, "Why is this happening to me and why can't get what I want?" The questions I should have been asking myself were, "What do I need to do to get out of this situation," "Who should I go to for help?," and "What is this situation trying to teach me?" When you ask better questions, you will get better answers. No matter what form of God you believe in, your life as an adult is your creation and your responsibility.

I believe in the law of attraction. I believe you can bring things into your life based on your thoughts, beliefs, and feelings; however, there are other laws at work, and one of them is the law of selfishness. I have heard some criticisms of the law of attraction. Namely, if, for example, something bad happens to an innocent child, is this the law of attraction at work? My response to that is we need to put the responsibility back on ourselves to ensure the safety and well-being of others, especially those who are the most innocent among us. Abuse of any kind is the fault of the abuser. It is not God's fault or the spiritual laws which are in place for our well-being. People hurting anyone for any reason, whether in the name of religion or selfish ambition, are not operating within the Spirit and essence of God. We are not justified in retaliation, only in protecting ourselves.

I believe we sometimes put God in the same category as people, meaning if someone does something bad to us, then God must act the same way with the same intentions as that person. A person may have bad intent, but God always has our best interests at heart, even though it may not feel like it to us. Believe me when I say God does not want us to hurt each other, but hurt people hurt people. We would rather hurt people than deal with our pain and none of us can see the extent of the pain we cause. We would rather blame God than face our wrong thinking and traumatic experiences. Just because your parents did not love you the way they were supposed to does not mean God does not love you. Just because you were in an abusive relationship does not mean God is abusive towards you.

I believe the saying, "When you know better, you do better." If we are constantly growing in our knowledge, how can we conclude we know better than the One who created the Heavens and Earth? In the book of Job, Job himself was lamenting about how Leviathan should swallow him up. And God was like, I don't think you want that Job, have you even seen Leviathan? I made him and he would tear you apart... Job was speaking about a situation he knew nothing of because of the enormity of his pain, remarkably similar to how a child thinks they know more than their parents. As we grow older, we realize we have even more to learn, and we do not know as much as we thought we did. Nor do we know more than God. Let me be the one to tell you God is not the cause of the problems you endured. Rather, God is the grace which carried you through those problems and was your strength to overcome them. God will fulfill his promises to you. It was hard for me to believe God was going to come through for me because of the way I had constantly been let down throughout my life by various people. I watched my friends and family struggle. I thought to myself, if God is not helping these other families, why would He help me? My focus was completely off. I then realized God has made a way for me numerous times before so why wouldn't He now? I shifted my focus from my disappointments to what God has done and was doing in my life. Another person's experience is not my lot. At the end of the day, I don't know why people are where they are.

I do not want you to live your life like I did, thinking of God as some distant callous creator who does not love nor care for you. I was able to see, for the first time, God has always been by my side helping me get through the troubles I had to endure and the self-imposed situations into which I got myself. God and people are separate entities. Religion comes from people; unconditional love comes from God. Without a doubt in my heart, I can tell you God loves you first and foremost. I know we hear God loves us so much all the time. We may believe He sent His only son to die for us so we can live. No matter how much I love any one person, I would never sacrifice my son for their well-being. The love of God is so strong and perfect He did sacrifice His son and He did it for you. Yes you, the person reading this book right now. Jesus died for everyone and even though you are part of the collective, He still would have done it, even if you were the only person alive. You are the apple of his eye, the person He looks at adoringly and will do anything for within reason and not at the expense of your well-being. God is not people. The purpose of Jesus dying is so that you could stop feeling bad about the things you have done and were done to you.

4. DID SOMEONE PASS AWAY?

death
(dĕth)
n.
The act of dying; termination of life.
The termination or extinction of something:

If someone close to you has passed on from this life, how do you live your life now that you have to live without them? I hope you know you are going to see them again, so how is the conversation between you two going to go? "Hey, since you died, I closed myself to the world, started self-destructive habits, and lived a miserable life because I decided to not do the work to heal..." I know once a loved one passes away, we are never the same, but how is destroying your own life honouring someone you loved who died? Are they looking down on you right now at you with their hearts filled with pride because of the way you are handling their death, or would they be deeply saddened by the life you are living? If it were you who passed away, would you want the people who loved you to live miserably because you're not there anymore? No, you wouldn't, so why are you doing it then? Who are you being self-destructive and depressed for? Clearly not for the person you've lost. Destroying your life because the person is not around anymore is harming no one but yourself. The person does not feel the effects of your self-destruction. Instead, one should make the deceased proud by living healthy lives. There are so many ways to honour people who have passed away, such as creating and naming your garden after them, creating a charity in their honour, finding out the ways they gave back to the community and keep their legacy alive in those ways. If roles were reversed, would you want the person/people you love to destroy their own lives because of your death? No, you would not.

I used to work in one of the hardest neighbourhoods in the West end of Toronto called Rexdale. Through an initiative put on by my church in partnership with the local police and politicians, the goal was to reach the troubled, violent youth of Rexdale to try and infuse positivity and hope into their lives so that it would minimize the shootings and deaths. I can only tell you of the unimaginable grief I experienced as I took part in the efforts to help. The gang violence is unbearable. I have never attended so many funerals in such a short period of time for black men who died as a result of gun violence. I attended nine funerals during one of the summers which were all for men who were murdered as a direct retaliation from a previous one. On and on it went, with no end in sight. I remember one young man gunned down as he was attending a funeral service at a church for his friend who had been gunned down. Gang violence is such a vicious cycle. If the victims of these murders could speak to us from the grave, they would tell everyone to stop. I am sure the deceased would tell their loved ones to finish school and make the best out of their lives and get out of the streets. Revenge does not ease the pain in any scenario. Gangs fulfill the quota to eliminate black men from this earth, nothing else. The same skills they develop to run illegal activities are the same skills they can utilize to be successful businessmen.

Every person who passes leaves behind lessons which they imparted upon us. At the time of writing this book, a local legend died in Toronto. This man was the first black man to own and operate a radio station here in Toronto geared specifically to Black and Caribbean audiences. He was known as Mr. G and I was blessed to have seen him in action, albeit for a brief time. Although I did not know him that well, his death had a major effect on me. He had so much more to give to this world. His radio station was only the beginning. I decided to honour Mr. G by completing this book and to make sure to execute the goals and dreams I have for myself as you never know when it will all come to a screeching halt. I have never seen a bigger turnout for a funeral in my life which goes to show how many lives he touched.

The question is not why a loved one had to die, but rather how you can you honour that person after they have passed away. Focusing on the injustice of any given situation is not going to help ease the pain, regardless of the circumstances surrounding the incident. I often hear the statement a parent should never have to bury their child, but repeating a statement like that to yourself can keep you in a state of suffering. How does a statement like that honour your child who passed away? Just ask the families who lose their children to gun violence or parents who lose their children to cancer or a million other ways. Parents lose their children every single day. There are no guarantees in life, and we are certainly not guaranteed to see our children outlive us. If you do get to see your children grow up, consider it a blessing. Every day you get to spend with your child is a gift.

I watched firsthand how my Tia Daisy forgave the person who took away her son's life in a car accident. Do not get me wrong, I do not believe it was a walk in the park for her. She grieved as any parent would do, but she did not let the grief destroy her as it would so many of us. Instead, she created a foundation in her son's name to help children in Latin America. Her son loved to take food to the homeless, so she now feeds the homeless for him. Will the pain ever go away for her? I am sure she misses him every single day. I cannot imagine the pain ever dissipating completely, but that does not mean she should ruin her own life and the memory of her son by living in the darkness and despair of losing him. That would not honour her son's life and I am sure her son would not want that for her. When my cousin passed away, I asked myself what lessons my cousin had imparted upon me. My cousin's death taught me to keep in better touch with my family because you never know when somebody will be called home. It really helped me to put aside some of the resentment which I had built up towards them.

Death can be unpredictable and cannot be controlled. It can only be accepted and grieved. My cousin Efrain died in his thirties, leaving behind his wife and two sons. The doctors had told his parents he would not live past his teenage years, but he lived long enough to be married and raise children. It showed me that even the best doctors cannot predict when we are going to die sometimes. Every death is tragic, but every death can provide a lesson to be learned.

5. YOU ARE NOT A LOSER

los·er

(lo☐o'zər)

n.

One that fails to win

A person who takes loss in a specified way

Nothing can diminish your worth. Not your age, not what you look like, not who your parents are, not the fact that your mother or father were not there for you during your childhood, or that they were there too much, not the person you dated, not the number of sexual partners you've had, not the degree or job you did or didn't get. You do not need anyone's permission to move on from your past and begin the process of healing and feeling better; however, if you feel like you need someone's consent, then consider this your approval to move on from your past and get yourself on the right track.

There is no benefit from mistreating yourself based

on your past mistakes. Everyone in this world has either been hurt or has hurt another person whether it was intentional or not. If, in your mind, you feel like you do not have self-worth, please remember you were not born with a sense of worthlessness and you have everything inside you to revive your innate positive value. Worthlessness is a learned behaviour and you can unlearn it the same way you learned it. We cannot go on beating ourselves up over things which have happened in the past, whether done to us or by us. Forgiveness (of ourselves or others) is a journey which involves a series of decisions we make to alleviate and eradicate the burden of the poisonous anger and resentment within ourselves of which we have yet to let go. You are always entitled to feel however you feel and you can go right on denying forgiveness to yourself or the people who have hurt you, but that poisonous anger and resentment will only keep contributing to your feelings of worthlessness.

You don't know this new me, I put my pieces back differently

I projected my negative self-esteem on the people around me because I did not like who I was. So, it became "they" did not like who I was. I eventually learned that what you believe people are saying about you is what you believe about yourself. They are you. Other people's opinions of you are none of your business and nor do they matter. What you think people are thinking about you is what you are really thinking about yourself. You are just projecting your thoughts onto them. What if you tried seeing your positive and beautiful qualities instead so you did not have to project your negative self-image onto others? If you know everyone has flaws, then you know everyone has good qualities, too. Once you truly start believing how exceptional you are with all your good qualities, you will see the good in others. That is when your perceived notion of other people's opinions becomes obsolete.

I often think of all the things in my life I was able to get through when I thought there was no way I could. Nobody gets to choose how they come into this world. You did not choose your parents, your siblings or family, the year you were born, or the country in which you were born for that matter. It is a fact of life that some of us get a head start in the race of life and some of us have to play catch up. If you can change your perspective on the possible shortcomings into which you were born and focus on what is inside you and the beautiful person you are instead of what you believe you did not get, then you win. Focus on what you want and how you are going to achieve it. Do not let it hold you back. Consider that the painful things which happened to you were because you are a light, because you are beautiful and completely amazing. Not the opposite.

Not everyone gets that picture-perfect childhood of living in a big, beautiful house being raised by two loving parents. If you were fortunate enough to have that growing up, then do not take it for granted because a lot of us did not get it. Just because there may be the appearance of a happy upbringing does not make it so; however, if someone you know did have that upbringing, be happy for them and be grateful you have an opportunity to be inspired to create that for your family if you choose to have one. Do not go out looking for the love your parents should have given you and try to find it in other people. If your parents did not give you the love you needed, give it to yourself. If your family did not give you the love you needed, create your own family with people who love and respect you. Also remember: people who had the picture-perfect upbringing can be just as self-loathing, unfulfilled, and unconfident as you are. Having a seemingly idyllic childhood does not guarantee that person moved or moves through life without suffering or adversity – they didn't choose how they came into this world either.

No matter what we may have had to endure throughout our lives, our value as a human beings will never diminish because God has not changed the way He sees you. You see yourself as damaged and He sees you as shiny and perfect. You see your life as over while God sees your life as just beginning no matter how old you are. You see yourself as worthless and He wants to give you everything. Just because there are people who made you feel like you did not deserve what you wanted does not mean you will not encounter people who will give you what you deserve with ease without making you feel you have to "earn" it. I want to let you know you are loved right now, no matter how you feel because feelings can be just as unreliable as people.

Our worth is not diminished with every mistake we make. This saying is so cliché but just like a $100 bill does not lose its value simply because it gets dropped on the floor, we have not lost our value just because we have gone through difficult times or because society says if certain thing happens, you are not worthy of a new beginning. We all deserve every good and beautiful thing this world has to offer despite what we have endured. The last thing you want to do is lose hope because it is hard to get it back once it is lost. Just know that if you have lost hope, you can get it back. I often reminisce about my poor mother who had to deal with my insanely rebellious ways growing up. The emotions inside us have to find their way out of us. I was rebelling against God, at least my concept of God, because deep down inside I felt worthless. I had built up so many walls around myself. I would not let anything in, including the love of those close to me, and nothing could get out. As a result, my heart grew numb. It has been such a long journey to find the hope and love I had lost, and I am ecstatic and grateful to be able to share it with you.

I mentioned before I believed nobody loved me or cared for me and I am here to tell you if you feel the same way I did, it is entirely untrue. You might sincerely believe nobody loves you because you are not being loved the way you think you should be loved, but this does not mean you are not loved. It took me most of my life to see the opposite was true. People can only love within their capacity and consciousness. My parents absolutely loved me in their own way, and I have family and friends and coworkers who absolutely love me, too.

I am writing this book because I genuinely believe if any one of my stories can help you, then the effort and experiences would have all been worth it. To recap, you have, at the very minimum, two conscious beings who love and respect you and I am confident in saying if you stop feeling sorry for yourself and really look around with gratitude at the people around you and the things you have, you would notice more people who love you.

The story of makeup artist Kevyn Aucoin is one which always broke my heart. His birth mother gave him up for adoption as a baby. Kevyn discovered he way gay at a very young age. His birth mother would not have taken kindly to his sexuality because of her religious and narrow ideals. Kevyn just could not get over the fact he was given up for adoption. He was crushed by the idea of it. He just could not see the bigger picture and why it turned out to be a good thing because he was given the tools to succeed with his skill and natural talent. Nevertheless, he could not get over the fact that his birth mother had abandoned him. He went on to become the biggest celebrity makeup artist in the world. You would see celebrities thanking him personally when they receive awards on stage. On set, he would tell the people he was working with how his mother gave him up for adoption for hours. He couldn't see that being given up for adoption was the blessing his natural mother never would have accepted him being gay. I wish for him that he could have seen his situation as a gift because who knows what would have become of him if he had not been put up for adoption? If you were abandoned as a child, it does not mean you are any less lovable than someone who was not abandoned.

If we have a void in our heart, it is our responsibility to fill that void with both God's love and the love we have for ourselves. If your parents abandoned you or if someone you loved and trusted broke your heart, let me tell you, you are more than fine. It is completely natural to go through feelings of anger and sadness. Sit in your feelings and allow yourself to feel them freely. It will not serve you to stay in those feelings. The key is to pick yourself up and move forward. Maybe the healing process includes reading a book or going on a trip to get away from it all. Or maybe it includes eating your favourite comfort foods. Or perhaps playing games on your phone and not answering any calls or texts for a short period of time. Do whatever helps you to engage in the healing process. With each passing day, you will see it is not as bad as the previous day. It might not seem like it, but you gained something good from every painful experience you went through. I am lucky enough to have amazing girlfriends and besties who have stuck with me exhaustingly through everything I have endured. Dria, Sharlene, Debbie, Cynthia, Cindy, Sandra, and Sonia: I love you ladies. I know through good times and bad, these alpha females will be with me, and I will be with them to the end of our lives. At a time when my family and I were estranged, God blessed me with female mentors at my church. If you feel like you are missing something, then God can replace what you have lost with something more suitable for you.

There is love all around you. The sun rises for you every morning and sets for you every night. The trees around you produce oxygen so you can breathe fresh air. Jesus died so you may live. So why are you not living your life to the fullest? People might say nasty things about you because they do not really know you or what is really going on in your life. If the reason I was fired from my high-paying VP job was so I could write this book for you and bring a new level of consciousness to tell you how amazing you are, so you can believe in yourself, it was all worth it to me!

6. THE REAL REGRET

re·gret
(rĭ-grĕt′)
v.
To feel sorry, disappointed, distressed, or remorseful about
To remember with a feeling of loss or sorrow; mourn:

The real regret will not be the guy who broke your heart or the dream job or business opportunity on which you thought you missed out, but rather it will be the dreams you chose not to pursue, the places you did not travel, the risks you did not take, the time you did not spent with people you love, or refusing to open your heart to someone who was deserving of it. For a long time, I thought I regretted having my son. A lot of women have a dream of what they want their family to look like and how their family is going to get started. You know what I mean, right? The partner and (maybe) kids, living in a nice house, maybe with a dog and a nanny, too; however, after completing some major soul searching, I came to the realization that what I really regretted were the circumstances which surrounded the birth of my son. The circumstances which included his father not being able to handle the pressure of staying in his son's life and scrambling for resources to properly raise a child.

"The mistakes I've made are dead to me. But I can't take back the things I never did." - Jonathan Safran Foer

We all make decisions based on the information we have at the time, as well as the state of mind we are in at that moment. You were always going to make the mistakes you made because of the level of experience (or maybe lack thereof) and information you had at that point of your life. Do not forget, you did not have the wisdom *then* which you have gained *now* because of mistakes you made *then*. We can tell ourselves we would have done things differently, but you could only have done things differently if you already had the knowledge you gained having resulted from making the mistake you made in the first place. Sounds confusing, right? All you need to know is you are now exactly where you are supposed to be. Things could not have been different.

I regretted getting married at such a young age because neither one of us were equipped to be married, but we tried, and I grew more into the woman I was supposed to be. I regretted all the years of effort I invested into men and women who did not appreciate me, but those relationships helped me to appreciate even more the people who do love me. I learned how to value myself because of those toxic relationships. For most of us, regret is simply a tool we use to punish ourselves over our perceived "failures." It is pointless to commiserate over the idea that our past would have been better if we had done things differently. Punishing ourselves is not going to change anything. I always regretted being with my ex-husband. I would always think to myself, "If I had been the woman I am today, I would not have even given him the time of day." What I recently came to understand was being with him is what helped me to become the woman I am today whom I love and am so proud to be. I now believe, in his own way, he did try to love me, but he was not equipped to handle me, especially since he was a man who had not dealt with his own trauma.

One of the things I love is hearing people tell their stories. One thing I hear a lot, especially from older people, is when they say the pain of regret is higher for the things they did not try, rather than the things they did try but did not work out. Think about this for a moment: if you try to follow what you believe is your dream at the time and it does not work out, you will hopefully learn a lot of lessons from that experience which you can apply to something new. Regardless, you still win. Is that not better than being tormented by the possibility of what could have been? If it does not work out, you can move on to the next challenge with enthusiasm and excitement which will bring you closer to the fulfillment you are seeking. Every part of your journey is preparation for the next chapter in your adventure. Your life is beautiful, you just need to decide to see it that way.

When it comes to the pain of regret, we always try to

overcompensate by going full throttle the next time around. It is during these times when we must remember the promise of God: He will give you blessings seven times over for your loss. Instead of being afraid you missed your opportunity, why not spend the time processing your perceived loss and do the work to be grateful for the lesson you took from that moment? Why not look forward to the next one coming your way with your focus on making the right decision? Regret is such a toxic emotion. You will never regret the lessons you have learned from your past experiences. Though it may have taken some time, it is never too late to start over. I started over at 36. My mother started over at 65 when, according to a Facebook comment she left on my page, she found herself only after she started to accept herself for who she is.

'If at first you don't succeed, try, try, try again.'

We only fail at something when we stop trying. If we keep trying, we are constantly working to become better versions of ourselves. If you are reading this book, it is an accurate assumption to say you are alive and breathing which means you still have an opportunity to change the things you dislike. If something does not go the way you planned, try again, only take a different approach to reach your destination and apply what you learned.

Wake up in the morning and greet the day like you would greet your best friend at the door. Live your best life today because you will never get today back. If you are in mourning, start to find the joy in your daily activities in honour of your beloved one who passed away. If you were fired from your job, start finding joy in your day by doing things you normally would not have been able to do because you will eventually find a better job. Opportunities will always be there for you.

God does not want us to merely survive our experiences; He wants us to unearth the wealth of information gleaned from these experiences and come out stronger. If you are going through something, you might as well get all the wisdom and understanding you can. Your mistakes, your failures, your disappointments, and all your experiences which cause you pain, guilt, or shame do not disqualify you from being worthy or living a good life. I want you to believe your experiences are equivalent to possessing all the jewels and diamonds in the world. Do not get caught up in the pain caused from past experiences.

What you have been through is not going to keep you from getting or being something or someone better. For example, if you were poor as a child, it does not mean you cannot or will not be rich as an adult. The only thing that matters is the present moment. The past no longer matters because it no longer exists. You are perfectly fine, even if it does not feel like it. You are no longer going through that painful experience; your soul is intact. You have grown from all your past experiences. You can handle anything that comes your way. I believe you can change this world by being the best version of yourself and by using the things you have learned from past experiences to help others. There is nothing wrong with feeling remorseful about certain things you may have done in your life. We all make mistakes, but you are not your mistakes.

You are so much bigger than them.

"Success is not final, failure is not fatal: it is the courage to continue that counts" - Winston Churchill

I am obsessed with Cardi B's song "Get Up 10." I cannot tell you how many times I have fallen, whether it was in my marriages, in my career, or as a mother, but I can tell you I always got back up. If Simon Cowell did not get back up, there would be no American Idol or X Factor. If Fergie did not get back up, there would not have been the Black-Eyed Peas as we know them. If Kanye West had not gotten back up, there would be no Yeezys or some of our favourite songs we cherish. Cardi B, Beyoncé, Michelle and Barack Obama, the Kardashians, Kelly Rowland, Nicky Jam, Adele, Jennifer Aniston, Jennifer Lopez, Walt Disney, George Foreman, Michael Jordan, Kobe Bryant, and anyone else you look up to have all had to get up after they fell.

7. YOU HAVE A PURPOSE

pur·pose
(pûr′pəs)
n.
The object toward which one strives or for which something
exists; an aim or goal
Determination; resolution

We hear the word "purpose" so often. I once went to a real estate conference, and I signed up for a "finding your purpose" seminar which was supposed to help me identify what I was put on this earth to do. I went to the workshop all excited about it and the seminar ended up being a workshop about email marketing. This was done by a person well known in the self-development sector. Even though her description for her workshop was misleading, what I got from her seminar was that there are numerous things we are put on this earth to do. I am going to try to do my best to articulate what I believe all our purposes are.

Your initial purpose is to master who you are. Figure out which of your problems are generational and which problems are yours. You can then do the work to heal and change them accordingly. I thought my problems with my mother were just a product of the issues between us because when you have an issue with someone, it is hard to have an objective perspective. The issues between us were so bad that we stopped speaking to each other for several years. After having conversations with certain family members, I realized the issues with my mother were generational within my mother's side of the family. My great grandmother had abandonment issues which she received from her mother, and she then passed them on to my grandmother who then passed those issues to my mother who then passed them on to me. I have a wonderful friend who is the Executive Director of a well-known charity for inner-city youth in Toronto who one day shared her own story with me about her relationship with her mom. Her story is hers to tell, but what resulted from it is it allowed me to open myself up to forgive my own mom. Breaking the negative generational mindset is part of you mastering your own life and healing your own trauma.

Just because you have learned to live with your trauma does not mean it is not affecting your life. I displaced the anger of my sexual abuse onto my mother. I blamed her for not protecting me against the babysitter who sexually abused me. After watching the documentary

Athlete A on Netflix and seeing what Larry Nassar did to those athletes and some of them right in front of their parents, I realized these predators are masters at concealing their horns. If Larry Nassar was able to sexually abuse these poor girls right in front of their parents, then what can a childcare provider or family member do? I did not even realize the rage I had towards my mother until a powerful energy therapy session I attended unearthed what I had buried. As a result of healing that part of me, I closed the doors on old, toxic relationships which were unknowingly counterproductive to my healing. There are times when solely changing external factors in our lives cannot close those doors alone and personal healing has to come from doing the work. I attained a coveted VP position in a company. I was hanging out with some of the most affluent and influential people in Toronto. I lived in nice places. I drove nice cars. None of these things dissipated my anger toward or healed my trauma involving my mother until I took the time for myself and put in the work to attend the energy therapy session. Self-development is also your purpose. Mastering our mental and emotional health through different forms of therapy, hard conversations, reading books, podcasts, and going to workshops and seminars is putting in the work. Becoming your highest self is your purpose.

I believe everyone is here to be of assistance/service to the people around us. The experiences from which we need healing are the very experiences which can be utilized to help and heal other people who have been through similar experiences. I was bullied in couple of the workplaces I previously worked, and I used those experiences to empower people who worked for me to develop a positive workplace environment. I wanted my team to be happy to go to work everyday. There are things you can do right now which can make a difference in someone's life. Say something encouraging, cook for someone going through a hard time, buy a homeless person a meal and do not judge them, perhaps take someone grocery shopping. Turn the pain you have experienced into purpose. If you were neglected as a child, make the people with whom you come into contact feel heard and valued. If you have been abused in the past, volunteer at a local shelter or, better yet, start a support group for those who are dealing with abuse. Identify what has brought you your pain and make it your purpose to assist in healing those who have gone through or are going through the same. Be the change you would like to see in the world. Exercise your purpose as a healer. Be that someone you wish you had when you were going through your struggles. I felt as though I did not have the wisdom and knowledge instilled in me while I was growing up. My mother's generation was a generation which did not necessarily talk about their past mistakes or what they had been through so I can understand why this wisdom was not passed on to me. Not receiving this wisdom forced me to garner it from different spiritual principles and different thought leaders whom I studied over the years. I used these principles to get myself out of the mess I was in and now I take what I have learned through my experiences to help other women through their problems. By helping these women at shelters and various workshops around Toronto, I turned my pain into purpose.

Never forget there is someone out there waiting for you to become who you were meant to be. They are waiting to be liberated. They need you to help them along their journey. There is nothing more inspiring than seeing a person do what they were born to do. Someone in desperate need may be waiting for you to write your book, produce your play, open your restaurant, start your YouTube channel, become an editor, become a teacher, nurse, or social worker, or to pursue whatever dream is in your heart. There are people in this world who are waiting for someone to come along and push them in the right direction by being an example. Be who you were born to be. There is something special about a person who guides another to the fulfillment of their destiny when they find the courage to be themselves and follow their own dreams. It is almost like a person being completely themselves gives someone else permission to be themselves.

Train yourself to focus on what you have instead of what has been taken away from you. If you keep moving forward, I promise, you will regain everything you have lost and then some. It is thought that Winston Churchill once said, "If you're going through hell, then keep going." Keep moving along through the murky waters. Keep going and never give up. One day, I assure you, it will all be worth it! What is your passion? What is that business idea or career move you think of every single day? For me, it has been motivational speaking. This is what I dream about doing with my life. Not a day goes by where I am not dreaming of speaking in front of people and empowering them. I visualize standing in front of a huge audience telling them how amazing I think they are and encouraging them to wake up every single day to strive to live their best lives possible. I do not regret how long it has taken me to reach that pinnacle because I have now put myself in a position to not only follow my dreams, but to realize them.

Your future and your purpose are bigger (and feel better) than the pain you experienced in the past. Your purpose is more important than the struggles which have gotten you to where you are. There would be no butterfly without a caterpillar. What if the caterpillar were afraid to go through metamorphosis because of what it thought people would think if they watched them hanging and struggling inside a cocoon? I would rather look like a fool following my dreams than look great not doing a damn thing. I currently watch my son as he pursues his dreams of photography. Allow me to take you back for a moment. It started at the age of four when he would declare to all who would listen that he was a man. He then decided to become a rapper, performing at his school and church. His path would quickly change as he then decided to be a drummer. Then, he made the decision to play soccer. Now, he has ventured off into the social media realm as well as photography and I could not be prouder of him. No one gets to their promised land without trying and going through detours, both of which are an essential part of the journey. Every single person on this earth has a purpose in life, and the circumstances surrounding your birth do not change that. Regardless of all the negative things you could list about your life, the truth is, you are a walking miracle. You are God's purpose here on earth. The things we have done and who we are, are two different things. We are who we are because God created us. Our actions are affected by our environment, our heritage, people who are around us and we are always growing in our understanding of what is right and wrong.

"Comparison is the thief of joy." -*Theodore Roosevelt*

2018 was a hard year for a lot of people I know personally. I remember a friend telling me she thought she was never going to get out of the situation in which she felt she was stuck. Because of what she said, I took notice of my own depressed energy. I was tired, but as tired, mad, and frustrated as I was, I had come too far to give up at that point. Remember, you only fail if you give up and I had decided I was not going to give up anymore. I will adjust my plan and refocus myself, but giving up is no longer an option, regardless of what my circumstances looked like. During the process of failing and trying again, you have a chance to honour yourself. Do not compare yourself to anyone else. One of the reasons why it has taken so long for me to pursue my purpose was because I was always comparing myself to other people. When I was growing up, I was not exposed to overly successful people. It was hard for me to push past what I was seeing because I did not want to stand out and be special. Comparing yourself to others is a death trap. It leads to irrational fears and guilt, along with perceived feelings of inadequacy. You are the only you and you cannot be anyone else. Every time you chastise yourself for something someone else is and you are not, you are telling yourself you are not good enough for something entirely out of your hands. Even if you were the things you're envying, you would never be them in the exact same way as anyone else. Be grateful for your own light and do not put it under someone else's shadow by comparing yourself in any way. Shine brightly on your own and the joy will come.

One of the reasons why people do not do well is because they make a conscious choice to not pursue their dreams. If God is the vine, they intentionally detach themselves from Him for whatever reason they may have. You matter, only for the simple fact you exist, and you are alive on this planet. You are beautiful, so start acting like the beautiful soul God created you to be. The world is not complete without you. You are a wonderful, amazing soul who has a purpose here on this Earth, so stop acting in a way which does not represent your awesomeness. In some shape and form, God will replace what you have lost.

"Whether you think you can or whether you think you can't, you're right"-Henry Ford

Add a little spice to your plan. Write down your goals, dreams and, with a nice glass of bubbly, invite your girls over for a girls' night and share with each other your aspirations. Create a vision board so you can look at it daily. I hope by facing my unfounded fear about writing this book, it will be used as an example for those reading to do the same. You already know what your dreams are. You think about them every day. If you are anything like me, you have been thinking about it since you were a kid. Do not misinterpret fear. Do not give up on the basis you think you are not good enough. I thought the same thing, yet here we are. You are holding my book in your hands and reading it.

Painful experiences are different for all of us. For some of us, it may be someone you love passing on from this world. For others, it might be dealing with the separation of your parents. Maybe it is being betrayed by your supposed best friend. We often frown on making mistakes because we are conditioned to think there is something seriously wrong with them. The truth is, the more mistakes you have made, the more life you have lived. When you start something new, like a job, or perhaps becoming a parent, or going back to school, you will inevitably make mistakes. Making those mistakes enables you to grow and learn. They help mold you into the best version of yourself. If you want to avoid mistakes, you might as well be living inside a padded room wearing a straitjacket because there is no chance on earth you can avoid them. Mistakes help to unfold your purpose. Things going wrong is just as much confirmation you are doing the right thing as things going right. Problems are always going to come up.

Your purpose will unfold continuously because your purpose is always evolving. As you heal your past and help people around you, especially if someone is enduring pain similar to yours, you will discover more of your purpose. God is always unfolding something new for you. Your legacy will be all the lives you have touched and are better people because you were on the earth and were brave enough to face your fears to do what was right. You might not like where you are right now but remember that Joseph was promoted as the second most powerful man from jail and David was promoted to King when he was a shepherd.

8. YOU HAVE TO SAVE YOURSELF

save
(sāv)
v.
To rescue from harm, danger, or loss
To keep in a safe or healthy condition

It is important you develop yourself and be there for yourself. Make sure you spend time focusing on your own life. Sometimes, we allow others to take advantage of us and sometimes, we take advantage of others. For years, my schedule was filled with things I had promised to do for others instead of things for myself. This led to deep feelings of resentment. These interactions were adding to the depression which had already crept into my life. This downward spiral (along with other factors) led to alcohol abuse, drug abuse, tolerating different forms of abuse from people, and a slew of other negatively impactful activities. I was helping others fulfill their dreams while completely neglecting my own. I do understand there are seasons to serve, whether it is serving your family, place of worship, or charity, but there are also seasons where you need to focus on yourself. You should help people with the fullness of your life, not with the emptiness of it. Putting yourself last is so 1980s.

I used to feel I never fit into any particular group, regardless of where we lived. I always excelled at sports because it helped me escape my reality. We moved around like we were a military family, but my parents were not serving our country. We lived in places where everyone was just trying to survive. I was never in the same school for more than two years. It was not until I was old enough to take the bus was I able to stay at one school for a long stretch of time. At that point, I opted to stay at the same school which, at one point, meant a two-hour bus ride. My sexuality was awakened at a young age by my babysitter as a toddler, so I was always looking for love and approval from others in the wrong places. I was more concerned with what people thought of me or what they were saying about me rather than focusing on healing my own pain, my own self-worth, and my own goals.

When I became serious about improving my life, one of the first things I did was to purge all the toxic people who were present in my life. I have dealt with and tolerated a lot of low-frequency people in my lifetime.

People say you should never burn a bridge, but I feel perfectly fine lighting one on fire. When I cut off a toxic person from my life, I noticed positive changes in my life immediately. I tolerated a lot of people who would blame me for things and create negative situations to overcompensate for what they were lacking and for their own trauma to justify the way they were treating me. Regardless of how great you are, people will always reduce you to how they want to treat you based on their feelings about themselves. When I cut those people off, things just got better for me naturally. I later found out that this process is called pruning. It is the same concept as pruning a flower. When you remove dead leaves from a flower, it causes the flower to flourish and brighten even more. I understand it is not that the flower will not experience pain during this process. It has to take care of itself by removing the dead leaves or petals which are leeching the nutrients out of it so it can be the best version of itself for a longer duration. The same goes for us. No, we are not supposed to be alone in this world; however, if people are taking advantage of you, not respecting your boundaries, keeping you in a negative state, do not hold you in high regard, or are always taking from you and leaving you empty (even if they are family), there might come a time when you will have to distance yourself from them until you are strong enough to be around them without feeling badly.

'You shall receive mercy, but ask for none'

I remember one time pondering the actions of these types of people. Then it hit me: these are all things I had done to others and myself. I rarely kept my word to myself or others. How could I feel loved by the people around me if I did not love myself? If you take the time to examine the problems you think you have with those around you, do not be surprised to see you have the same issues with how you view yourself. Remember how we talked about how people will treat you the way you treat yourself? Well, if people are not keeping their promises to you, then ask yourself if you are keeping the promises you have made to yourself and if you keep promises to other people. People might always have something to say about you and your life which is something you cannot control. Ask yourself what you are saying to and about yourself. Are you self-doubting? Do you not have confidence in your abilities? You will soon notice what happens around you reflects what is going on inside you. Change begins in places most people try to avoid. We manifest people who echo the way we treat ourselves. If we want to create change in our lives, we always start with change from within ourselves. If you do not have anyone in your life who appreciates and honours you, could it be you do not appreciate and honour yourself?

Hear me out. I am not saying you will not need help while you are on your journey to becoming the best version of yourself. At some point, everyone needs help. One of the personal disappointments I had in myself over the years was always looking for some form of external help more than looking to help myself. The moment I stopped looking for someone else to swoop in and save the day and looked inward to find the answer was a red-letter day in my personal journey. All it took was a teen pregnancy, failed relationships and friendships, and getting evicted from my home to come to this realization. Like I said, it comes easier for some than others.

I had a mentor who was able to help steer me in the right direction. He taught me the importance of being self-sufficient. For most of us, there is no prince on a white horse who is going to ride in to save the day like it is portrayed in your favourite fairytale. For most of us, we do not have a rich uncle who is going to leave us a big inheritance. You are going to have to be your own hero and the end of the story will be just as glorious and it will feel just as good. Think of the gratification you will have once you have succeeded. It builds your confidence and self-esteem and gets you ready to achieve more of your goals. You have the skills and attributes required to make money, buy a house, and live that peaceful life you want. It will feel all the more satisfying knowing you built this with your own two hands.

At one point, it felt like I was hanging by a thread. Just a little gust of wind would have forced me down into a black hole. Nobody in my life really caught on. I am simply not deserving of the grace I have been given from my higher power. I feel just being alive is an accomplishment. It may have taken over a decade to put the pieces back together, but through my faith in Jesus Christ I was able to do just that. Everyone is different. Some will find peace and fulfillment this way, while others might find it through other faiths, or other activities such as gardening, cooking, dancing, meditation, going for walks, or any other thing which fills their souls. Your life is a gift.

I do not care what people have told you. You are a precious gift and an invaluable masterpiece. Educate and protect yourself. Take care of yourself and if you do not know how, then ask Google. If you do not know how to use Google, learn. Ask those around you how they take care of themselves. Self-love and self-care look different for everyone, and you will find the answers once you start asking.

"For I know the plans that I have for you. Plans to prosper you and not to harm you. Plans to give you hope and a future."
- Jeremiah 29:11

You were always going to make mistakes. There is no avoiding them. You were always going to have to fight your way through those painful experiences because nobody is exempt. You were always going to make the mistakes you made because of the circumstances around you and the information you had at the time. They were inevitable. You learn and grow from your mistakes, especially when you start a new venture or are doing something for the first time. Some mistakes will be small and barely felt. Other mistakes will shake the foundations of your business or your relationship(s), or they will alter your soul completely. I genuinely believe, in the end, life will autocorrect itself and it will all work out for the better. In a world where people go through painstaking efforts to hide their mistakes and pretend to be perfect, it might seem like your mistakes are too big for you to bounce back from them. At some point in life, everyone has had to learn the hard way. Even the best people make mistakes. The next time you see a decidedly successful person, just know they, too, have made a lot of mistakes and are still making them. The big difference is when they fell, they picked themselves back up, got back on the saddle, and rode again. Only this time, they rode harder. They decided not to quit. You get a second chance, or third chance, or 200th chance, as long as you are alive. So please get back up and try again.

"Success consists of going from failure to failure without loss of enthusiasm" —Winston Churchill

Take the time to design the type of person you want to be and the life you want to live. No one is going to do it for you, only you know who you are supposed to be. If someone else were to do it for you, they would try to turn you into someone they think you should be. So please do it yourself and the right people will come along to assist you.

9. YOUR HAPPINESS IS YOUR RESPONSIBILITY

hap·py
(hăp'ē)
Adj.
Enjoying, showing, or marked by pleasure, satisfaction, or joy. Cheerful; willing

I was obliviously notorious for not wanting to take responsibility. Nobody was better at accusing other people or displacing anger than I was. Be careful of people that create their own drama and then think they are the victim. I can't say I was using any form of birth control, but I completely blamed the father of my son for having a child at the age of seventeen even though it takes two people to make a child. In the strangest way I believed that my parents were the cause for all the bad relationships I had and the rebellious attitude I chose to embrace. I was judging and criticizing others all the time, but the truth is, my resentment and bitterness focused my attention on other people, so I did not have to deal with my own issues. Matthew 7:3 says, "Why do you look at the speck of sawdust in your brother's eye and pay no attention to the plank in your own eye?" Consider when you point your finger at someone else, you have three other fingers pointing back at you. You do not have the authority to change anyone if you are guilty of the same thing that you are accusing them off. You cannot ask someone else to change in any form of a relationship if you are doing the same thing.

Here is a life lesson: as long as you are blaming someone else for the decisions you have made in your life, you are not taking personal responsibility for your choices. When you blame others, you lose the power within yourself to change your situation so you can cultivate the life you want to be happy. As an adult, everything you are lacking or everything you do not have ceases to be someone else's fault and becomes solely yours. As a child, it might not have been your fault that certain experiences happened to you, but as an adult, you are responsible for the way it continues to affect you.

Most people believe being protected, taken care of, and educated are fundamental rights which should be given by their parents. Even though these things are nice and beneficial, I think a lot of people do not get these things, especially not from their parents. So please stop beating up your parents for all the things you thought they did not give to you. You were never guaranteed a two-parent household with all the love this world had to offer, but the beauty of it is, you can learn to give this love and these opportunities to yourself now. Taking responsibility is understanding that as an adult, the onus is no longer on anyone else to make you happy. All it means is you are going to have to figure out how to get these things for yourself now. The kids who did have parents who helped them will eventually have to figure out how to get things for themselves as adults, so we all end up doing the same emotional work in the end.

I needed to forgive everyone I felt had hurt me in the past including myself because being grateful for your life and who you are is the foundation of being happy. You cannot hate yourself and your experiences and still be happy because you are your experiences. If you hate the experience, then you hate a part of yourself. Self-love can be muddy and uncomfortable at times and don't let anyone fool you about that. In order for you to be truly happy, you have to love yourself and love the things you have been through. This brings me back to forgiveness. I had gotten so comfortable staying angry at people. No matter how much I tried to run away from forgiveness, I exhaustingly kept circling back to the same lesson of forgiveness. When it finally won over my need to stay angry, I decided to change. In order to be happy, I had to surrender my negative emotions I had towards the people whom I perceived as having hurt me. As the saying goes, "Hurt people hurt people." I could not see how I was hurting people. When you harbour the hurt inside your soul it affects how you treat people and how you treat yourself. Often, it is easier to cause pain than to deal with your own. Instead of continuing to hurt people and muddle through life, I decided to forgive everyone including myself in the same way I would have liked to have been forgiven if the roles had been reversed. You cannot pretend to be a happy person and treat people poorly because genuinely happy people treat people well. I had to learn how to be happy and treat people well and I am still learning.

A friend of mine once told me men are like trains: if you miss one, another will be along in fifteen minutes; however, this does not apply solely to men. The best part of being at the station is that you get to decide which train you get on, whether it is a job train, a partner train, a friendship train, or any other kind of life train. The key is to be patient and get on the right train or you will end up somewhere you do not want to be. A wrong destination could make you try to turn something which is supposed to be temporary into something permanent. Instinctively, you know you are in the wrong place, but you try to "make it work." For example, on the relationship train, I have been married to some good guys who were just not for me, but I wanted them to be. Either people will treat you well and love you the way you need to be loved or they will not. You should not have to beg and fight to be loved. If the person is unable to or does not want to love you the way you want them to love you, there is someone out there who can and will. Everything which is meant to be will fit in the right place with ease, it might just take some time. Again, this is true of jobs, relationships, friendships, life. You will get on the right train. You are going to end up where you want to be, and I want to be here to help you make good choices.

10. HAVE YOUR OWN

own
(ōn)
n.
That which belongs to one

I have had the pleasure of meeting and working for a lot of successful businesspeople throughout my life thus far. The most common thing I heard from them was if they had waited for their success to be handed to them, they would not be as successful as they are now. Please… do not wait on people to change your life and get the things you want. The truth is you are capable of helping yourself in any circumstance. You can earn the money you need, create a plan to get out of debt, make the career changes and lifestyle changes. I have had help along the way, but people like helping people who are helping themselves. We all know what we want to do but make every excuse in the book as to why it cannot happen for us and why now is not a good time. Those who do not follow their hearts will have to face whatever force of nature comes along to redirect them to their true path. One experience which helped me understand this principle was having my employment terminated. Getting fired is embarrassing enough, but for me, it was why I was let go. Imagine warning people within the organization not to work with a con artist and then getting fired for what this con artist did. For at least a year prior to this incident, I had felt it was time to move on from that job position, but I made excuses for not leaving. The truth is, I was not following my passion. I was settling for jobs which would merely pay the bills and gave me a sense of status but did not provide any personal gratification.

You see, growing up, I never knew what it was like to have money. My mother was a single mother of three children, so money was always really tight. Coming from a place of low means, I can tell you how hard it was to keep the faith. I really struggled with the hope that, one day, I would have more than enough because it just seemed so improbable it would actually happen. I mean, how can someone wish for something they don't know exists or have never seen before? Sure, I wanted it to happen, I just did not think it ever would.

What took me a very long time to learn was that the power within you is powerful enough to knock down any barriers and elevate you into places and with people that you have not had to the chance to experience when you were growing up. There are of rags-to-riches stories of Barack & Michelle Obama, Oprah Winfrey, Denzel Washington, Sarah Jakes Roberts, Taraji P. Henson, Charlize Theron, Joyce Meyers, to name a few celebrities but the same is true for doctors, lawyers, business owners, judges... I could go on, but you get the point. Their journeys were not perfect or a straight line to achieving their dreams, but they did not allow their mistakes and detours to stop them from reaching their goal.

One of my proudest moments early on was when I acquired my first apartment for my son and me. A friend of mine thought perhaps there was someone paying for it which was not the case. I cannot tell you how proud I was to tell this person I had achieved this all on my own. I am not saying I have never received help along the way, but my goal is always to be self-sufficient. There is just something about acquiring something with the money you earned with your own hard work and effort which feels that much better than the gratitude you would have if someone had given it to you. The self-gratification you receive from providing for yourself is stronger and longer lasting than fake friends and materialism. It is an unapologetic confidence which will straighten your posture and have you looking people in the eye.

Do not ever feel like you have to live up to someone else's expectations or follow in another's footsteps. I have always sought to help women. I started doing workshops with women at a local community church I was attending at the time with my friends Sharlene Khan and Cherise Lewis. I transitioned to supporting workshops at various shelters around the city, but, deep down, I was not satisfied. It was at that point I teamed up with a friend to create a website, findyourbeautiful.com. I collaborated with Anna who created a website for me to be able to reach women through a different medium. This was followed up with a women's online empowerment movement I worked on with a business associate which featured an online magazine written for women by women. We were reaching women all over the province of Ontario, completing workshops in schools for various charities and executing various lifestyle events. My passion is to encourage women to live the best lives they possibly can. This passion would not have been discovered if I had not gone through the experiences I had. I created this path for myself because no one around me was doing it. My journey was born out of feeling that women were expected to be perfect without given the proper tools to succeed. I created my own lane by doing what I love to do, and I expect you to do the same.

11. DO NOT BECOME THE THING YOU HATE

hate
(hāt)
v.
To feel strong dislike for or hostility toward
To feel dislike or distaste for

We have all wanted to get back at a person who hurt us at some point. If someone cuts you off in traffic, does it mean you can do it back? A former boss of mine would pay his employees peanuts and his justification for doing so was he himself was paid a minuscule wage when he was younger. If someone is unkind to you, why would that justify you being unkind to someone else? These types of experiences we endure are there to teach us what not to be, but people take it as a pass to become the monster that they hate. Being the bigger person is hard at first, but if you persist it will eventually become second nature and feel amazing. There are blessings which come with being the bigger person. There are also blessings which unlock at each level of your character as you grow from each experience.

Nowhere in the bible does it justify being nasty in response to a person, but I do not believe in being a doormat for anyone either, so try to find a balance. This does not mean do not stand up for yourself if you believe someone is attacking you. It simply means you do not have to lower yourself to someone else's level to get your point across or that you cannot move on from an unjust situation.

I look at it this way. Either you can choose to get 'revenge' and stoop to their level or take the high road and watch their hearts break.

Everyone deserves to be treated with kindness, respect, and dignity, so make it a habit to start treating people that way, whether at home, work, or in social settings. Do unto others what you would have done unto you. This is known as the "golden rule" to most, or as a verse from the gospel of Luke. Regardless, it is something for which we, as a society, should strive and not just when things are going great but even (and perhaps especially) in the times which give us the most pain and reason to be less. In those times, be more.

Some ill-willed people may pull these stunts on you just to elicit a response. Beyoncé says in one of her songs, "the best revenge is your paper," and she is talking about how your success is the best way to get back at people who try to bring you down. Daymond John says the best revenge is to love yourself. Let the painful circumstances you go through turn you into a better person, not a bitter one. Do not let negative experiences turn you into the person who hurt you. It only takes an instant to become bitter, but it will take you a long time to climb out of that hole. When something painful or negative happens, only you get to decide how you are going to respond to that situation. We are hard-wired to want to have relationships with others, but often we get hurt which causes us to turn away from the social interactions we want to experience. The right relationships can change your life for the better. Other people can inspire you to become a better person and add value to your life. Any relationship, whether in business, friendship, family, or love which makes you feel badly about yourself needs to end. I am not just speaking about abusive relationships, but rather ones which just seem to bring you down. Ending these relationships may hurt at first, but once you do, it will naturally make you into a better person. For me, the act of ending these relationships allowed me to be more productive and focus on other things which would improve my life. Trust what your gut is saying about others. The wrong people in your life can stop blessings from coming your way, just like the right people can be a blessing to you and make your life better. There are good people in this world; however, sometimes you need to get rid of the old, negative energy first before the new, better energy enters. You need to see examples of people being the bigger person and reacting in ways from which you can learn to improve your life and not adopt people's self-sabotaging practices so you can grow.

Don't use your past as an excuse to mistreat the people who are trying to care for you in the present – Michell Barker

In order to heal, we have to be able to admit our own disappointments because if you do not, you are going to end up expressing them through bouts of rage, addiction, depression, and manipulation of others. You might even repeat the very same disappointments which got you to this state in the first place, or you might repeat the same disappointments you saw in your parents which you vowed you would never do. We started out this book with this verse in Proverbs which says, "As a man thinketh in his heart, so is he." The thoughts we have in our hearts will manifest into reality. Some of us would rather bury this disappointment deep within us and live a toxic life than acknowledge it and let it go. When we get disappointed, we would rather get angry at people and lash out instead of communicating our hurt to them. I know vulnerability is not easy for everyone, but it is interesting how we would rather inflict pain and release our toxic energy on other people than properly deal with our own issues.

Do not despise what you have had to go through and what has made you a better and stronger person because of it. In the same way you do not regret an outfit that other people might have not liked seeing on you, do not regret a single thing which has happened to you. A close friend of mine lost his father when he was only two years old. A tragic story which would affect anyone, but the pain of not having a father helped him to become one of the best dads I have ever encountered. He could have, like many men and women, forfeited his responsibilities because he did not have a father, but he decided that not having a father was going to make him a better dad for his kids. He took the loss and made it into a gain by choosing to be a great father, not because he was set up to be one.

12. KEEP GOOD COMPANY

com·pa·ny
(kŭm'pə-nē)
n. pl.
One's companions or associates
The state of friendly companionship; fellowship:

I have been talking about the relationships between people all throughout this book because I learned the invaluable lesson of having good people in my life the hard way. Eckhart Tolle brilliantly tweeted the following, "If her past was your past, her pain your pain, her level of consciousness your level of consciousness, you would think and act exactly as she does. With this realization comes forgiveness, compassion and peace." When people judge others, it is because they do not know the person they are judging. If people are harsh towards you, it is because they do not know you. If they knew you, they would be forgiving, compassionate, and peaceful toward you. Follow your gut feeling. I would always get fooled by people because they would look alright and tell me they were my friend, but their actions did not align with what they said. I cannot comprehend how people will pretend to be a friend just to hurt or use someone. There are people who do not have empathy or remorse who will come into your love life, business life, and personal life to try to steal your energy. Watch out for narcissists. Read articles and watch videos on YouTube about narcissists so you can identify them when you encounter them in your life and also so you can understand the devastating effects of these types of people and how to recover from them. They will pretend to be an amazing human being and, at first, they will make you feel important and then over time they will start diminishing your worth. Everything will start becoming your fault and nothing you do will ever be good enough. I am oversimplifying how toxic and damaging these relationships can be because it took me years to recover from some of them.

Have you ever spent time with someone and found you felt horrible afterwards? You think to yourself nothing in particular really happens while spending time with this person, but for whatever reason you just feel like crap every time you leave their company. If people have good intentions, you will feel it. I find this to be true for me, personally, as well. Pay attention to people's actions more than their words. When I stopped communicating with these types of people, I could not help but feel a sense of relief. If your friends are never there for you and they seem to always be taking and not giving, let them go for now. There are people in my past whom I loved and deeply miss, but I know I cannot go back because the relationships were toxic. I am in a place where I want to love and honour others while, at the same time, love and honour myself. You are always going to have love for ex-best friends or ex-partners. That does not really go away, but you will gain a deeper love for yourself and your own life as a result of letting them go from your life no matter if they are family or regardless of how many years of friendship are between you.

If you are not being appreciated at work for the effort you are putting into the company, create an action plan to get out and find somewhere else you will be appreciated. The job market is too broad and there are too many companies which need good employees locally and internationally for you to tolerate not being treated well in the workplace. Finding the right job is similar to dating: you don't always find the right fit on the first try. You have to try a few things before you find 'the one' and you don't have to settle for the wrong one just because it's paying the bills.

The bible says if you grieve toward your brother, speak directly to the person, and if nothing comes out of that, you should then involve other people. If that does not work, then treat that person as an unbeliever. This is the same bible which says we are to forgive, but it does not say to waste our time on people who continue to hurt you. It is okay to speak to your partner and people in your life about the things which bother you. On the flip side, if we take issue with every little thing, people will just get tired of you and will not take what you are saying seriously. Address things which are most important to you like safety, cleanliness, traditions, or values and let everything else go. People cease to take a person seriously if they are constantly having a problem.

God is always with you, and you are never alone. It is okay if your life did not turn out the way you had hoped. It is okay to say you are disappointed if something did not turn out the way you expected. In this life, you are going to be disappointed a million times and by a list of all the people ranging from friends, family and people you encounter day to day. I felt nobody was really equipped to handle me. I even had a therapist quit on me. Only God could help me. He had to put certain people in my life who could not only handle me but could help me navigate through the pain and issues I had. Some people who helped me were super patient and loving. Some were wise and shared their experiences with me, while others were tougher and had to give me tough love, but it was love, nevertheless. You will get the people in your life you need to awaken your consciousness to who you are and what you purpose is, not necessarily the people you want.

While writing this book, I was going through my

own trials. I took a summer to reflect on my life, and to decide which path I was going to take to reach my goals. I decided to take an entry level job so I could finish writing this book. This book has saved my quality of my life. It did not matter what the circumstances were, God knew I needed a break. With all the traumatizing things which had happened to me, I never really took time to myself to sort through it all. I was working on myself, but God went deeper this time. This book has helped me work through more. Writing this book helped me to remember the sexual abuse I endured by my babysitter which I blocked out so I could finally deal with it, and once I started, my capacity to be openhearted increased. I was able to be loving towards the people in my life.

During this time, I fell in love with listening to podcasts. There is one podcast from Elevation Church called "Come Out Drippin." What I came to understand from listening to this podcast is God told Moses to look back at the Egyptian army which had been following the Israelites one last time before crossing the Red Sea. The Egyptians were trying to recapture the Israelites in order to reclaim the jewels and precious commodities the Egyptians gave them and to re-enslave the Israelites. The Egyptians wanted their wealth back, but they were unsuccessful. In this instance, Pastor Furtick was talking about our experiences as being precious jewels and how the devil wants to make you forget what you have learned. The devil wants you to go back to the negative state you were in before your enlightenment. Every experience you go through makes you stronger not weaker. There is both knowledge and wisdom and a wealth of information which can be gleaned from every experience we go through. If you look back at your past experiences and learn from them, you will release the negative energy brought on by those past events. These situations are there to prepare you for what is ahead, regardless of how painful or humiliating it was. The lessons we learn are the wealth we accumulate and honouring ourselves and others is our advancement in life.

We do not always reap in the same places we sow. I have sown time, effort, patience, money, resources, connections, and being the bigger person in some relationships with one person - or job - who never reciprocated my efforts, but then ended up meeting someone new, or finding a new position, and have had them treat me the way I wanted to be treated, or even treat me better than I expected. If you could just look at your past and what you have been through, no matter how hard it was, just know it was a time of sowing your seeds of growth, wisdom, and greatness. Be assured you will reap what you have invested in this planet, the people around you, and the jobs you have. Also remember, you may not necessarily reap where you think you should reap, but rather where the Universe would have you reap in a better field. Some of the people or jobs in which you have sown do not always have the capacity to let you reap. If you can look at your pain as a down payment on your blessing like I did, then and only then, will you find your happiness and be unstoppable.

13. THE LIES OF MOTHERHOOD

moth·er·hood
(mŭ*th*'ər-ho☐od')
n.
The state of being a mother.
The qualities of a mother.

I had my son at age seventeen years old. The whole experience created layers of regret and trauma. Instead of enjoying motherhood, I spent time focusing on how unfair my situation was and instead of seeing the beautiful boy I now had in my life. Girls were getting pregnant at age thirteen. I always told myself that would never be me, but I ended up getting pregnant at age sixteen. There is nothing new about teenage pregnancy. You see teenage girls pushing strollers down the street all the time. They are the brave ones who had enough courage to have their kids, but unbeknownst to them, they will be judged, criticized, and written off for their brave decision to keep their child. Anytime I tell someone I have a son and I reveal his age, I always get the "You look too young to have a child!" line, which is always followed by the 'I feel sorry for you' look. I am not sorry for having him. Yes, he drives me crazy, but I look at how Elijah has blessed the lives of others and I cannot picture this world without him. If criticism, judgement, and dirty looks are the price I had to pay to have him, then so be it. I decided to have my baby. I always found it interesting how most parents would tell their girls to avoid getting pregnant but would not mention the dangers of rape or drug abuse. Teen pregnancy seems to be up there with going to jail and getting a criminal record when it comes to things you should avoid. I was written off by many who should have been supporting me. My former teachers were telling the other students my life was essentially over. My basketball coach was telling a friend of mine I had no future. He was saying my life was headed straight to the gutter. Can you imagine teachers saying these things about their students? On a side note, that same basketball coach ended up in jail for robbing banks, so maybe he should have focused more on his own issues instead of criticizing me. People will always find time to attack and berate you, even if they are worse off than you. When you go against the grain of conventional standards of society, be prepared to be attacked. For me, that was just the beginning of my story and not the end. Situations might occur which drastically alter your life, but life will go on regardless.

I was not the only woman who was pregnant in her teenage years, but I am one of the few who had the baby at that time. I can remember driving my friends to their abortion appointments. I am not saying I have not had one after I had my son, but in reality, in this day and age, you have either had an abortion or know someone who has. You feel guilty if you have the baby and you feel guilty if you do not. You either deal with the relief you are no longer tied to the person who got you pregnant or you struggle through a lifetime of being responsible for another life for which no book or seminar can prepare you but will give you a greater purpose than yourself. I do understand the relief which comes from having an abortion, but are we not all here because someone chose not to abort us? I mean, why are we even with people who would inspire us to have an abortion? I know situations are more complicated than that. Ask yourself, "If I got pregnant by this person, would I keep it?" If the answer is no, then why are you wasting your time? If you have had an abortion, please go to counselling to work through the issues which got you to that point in the first place. I am empathetic towards women who have abortions. I believe some women who have them are haunted by the idea of their aborted child they will never get to see. I have had abortions after I had Elijah and even though I am ok with my decisions, I have never felt quite the same. I really believe that because women are so awesome and are such great nurturers, nobody grows up thinking they are going to have one. This is one of the unspoken experiences no woman ever wants to go through. It is up there with experiencing a miscarriage or being in an abusive relationship. It is easy to say they should never let it happen, but if we do not walk a mile in that person's shoes, we should be more empathetic and compassionate towards them. There is a journey that leads to every moment.

When my son was born, I did not connect with him right away. I remember my church mentor was like Michell, just hug him for 10 seconds like count to 10 and at first you will hate it, but over time it will feel natural. She saw something was wrong, but she did not approach me by attacking me. When I came to her house, she made me some tea, had lunch waiting for me, and addressed me with a solution. It was what I needed to hear at the time, and I learned how to hug my son which was the catalyst for me opening up more as a mother. Being maternal does not come naturally to everyone, but you can learn how, and the feelings will come.

And those feelings did come. Along with them came the guilt. Having "mommy guilt" plagues every parent. I cannot imagine there is even one mom who does not feel guilty about some aspect of their parenting. We fear in some way we are going to screw up our kid and the truth is that every parent does traumatize their kid in some way. Children have an amazing way of feeding off that guilt. Almost every child makes their parents feel like what they did was not enough. As a mom, you have to set boundaries with your children as well, reassure yourself you are doing the best you can. We, as mothers, tend to put ourselves last, but this attitude does not help anyone. As mothers, we have to take care of ourselves so our daughters will see the standard of what a strong and beautiful woman is, and our sons can have an example for what to look for in their partners. Learn to think only kind and loving thoughts about yourself. Filter out the bad ones. Put yourself first because nothing prepares you for motherhood. You may have to go at this all alone and be your own cheerleader, but you can do it (and do it well) all by yourself.

I feel as though moms, undeservedly, often get the short end of the stick. When you become a mom, it is almost like people only see you as the child's mother and nothing else. You are expected to give up your whole life and become a zombie-like creature who only tends to their little ones and nothing more. In some families, you almost cease being a person. I might be exaggerating for effect, but I do not think it is far from the truth. You are told you should not go out and have fun with your friends or you should watch how you dress. Live your own life. Every parent needs "me" time, whether it is a night out with friends, exercising, or whatever brought you joy before you had your kids. Do those things, even if people around you might think otherwise. Every little action gets scrutinized and criticized. As a mom, be prepared to receive criticism from all angles. Everyone has something to say or advice to share, especially those who do not have kids (they seem to be the most opinionated about parenting). I was at a baby shower one time where there was a little game the guests could play. There was a card and you had to write down whether you thought the baby was going to be a boy or a girl and suggestions for a name. The card also wanted the guest to write down a small piece of advice. I wrote, "Don't take advice about parenting your child from people that don't have kids!" When the hostess read my answer out loud, I received a lot of dirty looks from the childless guests for the rest of the night. Receiving advice is far more comforting when it comes from people who are raising children rather than people who are not. Get acquainted with other parents so you both have someone to lean on who are raising kids just like you. I am fortunate because my girlfriends had kids around my son's age, and they were incredibly helpful at giving accurate advice.

I never wanted to be a single mother. The thought of my son growing up not being raised by both his mother and father in one household was heartbreaking another layer of trauma I was holding. I dealt with this depression the only way I knew how: with excessive drinking and partying. I was a divorced, single mother who felt unloved and unwanted. It felt like everything which could have gone wrong with my life did. All my worst nightmares came true. I had to learn how to pull myself out of postpartum depression because no one knew what it was. So, they would see things I was doing and would attack me instead of asking me if I was ok. One night, I vividly remember sitting in my kitchen alone in the dark. On the kitchen table lay a knife. I remember feeling this deep feeling to end my life. It was at that exact moment I felt a very gentle nudge lifting me out of that dark place, letting me know everything was going to be okay. Suicide was not the answer that night, but suicide is never the answer. Who would look after my son? His father was not in his life so the responsibility of raising him was left up to me. I did have some help from my mother, but I did not want him to be looked after by her either.

I can tell you from experience not to believe the guy who says they will stick around after the birth of your child. I fell for it, and I know women who had it even worse. You should believe a man's actions more than his words. Examine how he is treating you and if his words align with his actions. If he makes a promise to you, does he keep it? How does he treat you? How does he treat the people in his life? This statement rings true with any job, any partner, or any family member, including your parents. Do not be fooled by what people say. Make sure their actions line up with their words. Relationships are meant to be give and take; however, if you are giving more than receiving and feel taken advantage of, it might be time to set some boundaries. Do not ever be afraid to prune off any toxic relationship.

I can still remember the night I received a Facebook message from the father of my son asking me for forgiveness. I remember reading how grateful he had been to me for raising Elijah without him. Let us not forget this man made my life a living hell for a period of time right after my son was born. At the time my son was born, he had told me he was going to be active in my son's life, but he was not. His child support was almost non-existent, and he was never reliable when it came to his weekend visitations. It seemed to be a regular occurrence, to the point where I would always have a backup plan in case he did not show. Becoming a mother has changed me in a very painfully beautiful way. This was not how I envisioned how my family would be. It took me over a decade to forgive him, but I did forgive him. He was already forgiven by the time I received his Facebook message. When I look back at this, I now firmly believe if his only job had been to convince me to have my child, he played the role he needed to in my life story. Why? Because, in the end, I ended up with a beautiful, chubby baby boy. Changing my perception of the circumstances allowed me to release the pain enough for me to forgive him. At the time, it bothered me to no end how there were people who promised they would help me raise my son, yet once he came into this world, they all vanished without a trace. This was the beginning of what showed me how to become a person of my word. Being a parent is going to completely change you as a person. It is going to give you a deeper understanding of the judgements you might have towards your own parents. Your kids are going to call you on your nonsense. Being a parent is a marathon from which you never get a break, and YOU GOT THIS.

Instead of being ashamed of what you've been through, be proud of what you have overcome - Dr. Phil

Children are truly a blessing and the experience of being a parent will change you in ways you never knew possible. Being a parent will push your physical and emotional boundaries in ways you did not know you could be pushed. It will bring both good and bad people into your life, so be prepared to sort through and eliminate the bad ones. There will be pain and heartache. Know that parenting is one of the toughest and thankless roles a person can have. It does not matter how many books you read or thoughtful blogs you subscribe to online, nothing can prepare you for the sleepless nights and restless days of motherhood. There will be those people who will want to label you as just a mother and nothing more. You will be invisible to some, but do not let anyone ever push you into a corner. I want to remind you: you will always be wonderfully you. You were beautifully you before you became a mother so figure out how to be beautifully you with your kids.

14. IN ALL THINGS BE GRATEFUL

grate·ful
(grāt'fəl)
adj.
Appreciative of benefits received; thankful
Expressing gratitude

Six months after I had just completed one divorce, I jumped into another relationship. Four years after that, I was in the process of completing my second divorce. This transition had left me emotionally, spiritually, and financially broke which meant I had to move back in with my mother for the second time because I could not afford my own place. At this point, I frustratingly searched for what I should do next and how I could level up in my life. I came across the movie 'The Secret' on Netflix which, surprisingly, helped me to understand gratitude better. I did not search out to understand gratitude but out of everything they talked about in the movie that is what stood out to me the most.

Practicing gratitude at the beginning, however, proved to be challenging because even though there are always things to be grateful 100% of the time like your breath, a roof over your head, and being able to hear and see, there was not one grateful bone in my body, but I decided to go for it and try to shed the thanklessness anyway. Practicing gratitude when I didn't want to was the best place to start practicing it because it eventually created in me the discipline of gratitude. So now I know how to be grateful when things are bad just as much as when they are good. Anyone can be grateful when things are going well, but it takes a person who is serious about changing their life to learn how to be grateful when they are not where they want to be in life. Being grateful for what I had and focusing on the good things which happened did allow me to start seeing positive changes take place in my life. Was it that good things started to happen or was I merely recognizing the good things I already had? No clue. The problem I had was staying consistent with this new positive practice. It seemed to me that as I went on this new journey, I would go through stages where I stopped being grateful and lose the progress I gained. Even with all this newly gained positivity I had developed, with all the results which continuously appeared, I would still, at times, struggle with keeping up with the practice.

Gratitude is the foundation of your happiness. Gratitude is a decision to be grateful the things in your life you appreciate. Gratitude will rewire your brain by focusing on the good you have in your life. Most people have a very materialistic view on how to obtain happiness.

You think to yourself, "If only I could land that dream job," or, "Once I am able to get my hands on that stylish new car with all the new features or live in that coveted area code, I will be happy." Whether you think you need that new home, more money in the bank, that fancy car, or even your "true love" to be happy, have you really decided not to be happy until you have those things? What about the time in between now and having those things? I am not saying those things are not nice to have, but ask yourself this: if it takes you ten years to get your dream house, does that mean you are not going to be happy for those ten years while you are in pursuit of it? Part of having free will is that you get to decide when at what makes you happy. The truth is these things may bring you a period of happiness, but it will never be long-lasting or deep. This is because it is not the job of these external things to make you happy. That job belongs to you. In my heart, I decided I was not going to be happy until I achieved what I wanted to achieve; however, when I achieved some of those goals, I was still a traumatized, unhappy person. My hopeless, unfulfilled state did not change one bit when I acquired a VP Position. The same can be said for when I moved into my beautiful new condo, got my brand-new car, or when I thought I met a great guy or when I had my son. After all that, I was still so unhappy that I continued to self-medicate with alcohol and sex because those things did not change the fact that I hated my upbringing and my life. These things did not change the story I was telling myself.

Be grateful now, even if you are not where you would like to be

With everything in life, practice makes better, and gratitude is best practiced every day. When I wake up the morning, before I even get out of bed, I start being grateful for things in my life even if I know my day is going to be challenging and tough. The definition of discipline is the practice of training to obey rules or a code of behaviour even when you do not feel like doing it, you do it anyway. So, everyday throughout the day, I say what I am grateful for even if I am having a bad day.

In this regard, I started being grateful for the people I loved, but also for the people who hurt me as part of my journey of forgiveness toward them. When you are grateful for the people who have hurt you, it releases negative energy you are holding toward them which makes room for more positive energy to flow through you. Please do not get me wrong, you are not grateful they hurt you, but you are grateful for the lessons you have learned through your interaction with them, and you are grateful you survived and overcame their experience. You can also be grateful they are no longer in your life. You do not want the people who have hurt you to "win" the situation by staying in a state of anger and hurt because they win if you do. The best revenge will always be to love yourself and be successful and happy in your own life. Redemption plays a role in living life to the fullest, but do not always go looking for redemption from others. You must find it within yourself and from your higher power. There is a verse in Isaiah 54 which speaks of our vindication which comes from the Lord and our battlements made of rubies and walls made of precious stones. The lessons we have learned are our precious stones which we can use to empower the rest of our lives. If your focus can be on what you learned and be grateful for it, you are either getting through the situation or have gotten out of the situation. Let me tell you, you have won the battle no matter what it felt like while you were going through it. Not everyone makes it but you have.

The bible says in all things be grateful. This means even if you have not landed your dream job you can be grateful for the one you have because, at the end of the day, you are employed and receiving a steady paycheck. Let's face it, having some of your bills paid is better than having none of your bills paid. Being grateful does not mean you are going to settle with what you have or that you cannot be ambitious and change your circumstances, but it does help you to enjoy your journey and not let people or things affect your mood as much.

Be grateful for who you are because it is utterly exhausting to try to be anyone else. Do not wish to be someone else but be happy for others. Remember, you do not know where their journey has taken them. I believe if you want what someone else has, you will also bring with it the journey they had to go through in order to get it. Are you willing to go through the pain and hardships they did in order to get what they received? I remember a time where I would be envious of what other people had, but at the same time, when I achieved what they had, it did not make me any happy. I finally realized where all this envy was coming from: I was not taking care of my own life the way I should have been. If you feel envious of what someone else has, you need to examine your own life in that area. If you have time to be envious about someone else's life, your time is not being spent taking care of your own business. There is nothing wrong with being inspired by someone else's life, but it should motivate you to go after your own desires and wants, not someone else's.

Gratitude might come easier to some people than others, I have no doubt about that. Here is the thing, though: if I can do it, so can you. It hurt my head at first to refocus on the positives and be grateful. It felt inauthentic, slow, and ineffective. I had to fight through these feelings of falseness and focus on being grateful in all situations until it felt organic to me. Life is not about being happy for a moment. Life is about being joyous even in times of distress and enjoying the journey to our next destination. It is about finding meaning in people and experiences which can be easy to overlook. It was hard for me to be grateful for the things I did not enjoy or did not want, but when I pushed through that initial deterrence, I could feel the positive energy rise from deep inside me while the negative energy slowly withered away. Life is not about being happy only when you get what you want. You are allowed to be and can be happy regardless of what you do or do not have. I am speaking to you as much as I am speaking to myself here, as I wholeheartedly believe gratitude is truly the key which unlocks the door to our happiness and enjoyment in life. This is coming from someone who once told God, "I am not going to be happy until I get what I want!"

I would always worry about money, especially being a single mother. I wanted to stop worrying, but did not stop until God showed me I could replace worry with gratitude, which I have since utilized many times. When I feel like worrying, I start listing all the things for which I am grateful, a simple exercise which brings me the relief I need. You can replace worry with gratitude because God has made a way and gotten you out of situations many times before. He still provides for you and will continue to provide for you in the future. You have what it takes to get through and overcome any situation that comes your way.

You can replace worthlessness with gratitude by being grateful for who you are, for who God made you to be, and for what you already have instead of worrying about what you do not have. You have something to be grateful for every minute of every day if you are brave enough to face it and acknowledge it. Change yourself and you will change your life. You got this.

You Are Not the Only One

ABOUT THE AUTHOR

Michell Barker has been empowering women in any possible way she can for the past 18 years of her life. Born in Panama, her mother and siblings moved to Dallas, Texas. At the age of three, Michell's family immigrated to Toronto, Canada. Daughter of Isabel Bejarano and William Vicente Barker, she watched how her mother overcame a society vastly different than the one she experienced back in her native El Salvador.

Through the church she was attending, Michell finally decided to take her self-development seriously when she decided listen to motivational speakers online, read countless books on the topic, and serve her church in any way she could. It was at this point, Michell decided she wanted to help women by sharing the lessons she learned which helped her through her journey of healing. At her church, with the help of Sharlene Khan, Michell started a girl's ministry called Daughters of Zion, which was based on scripture from the book of Isaiah. This ministry lasted for two years.

Michell then shifted her focus from helping women in the Church to assisting in women's shelters, as well as various women's groups and organizations around southern Ontario. It was at this time Michell started an online women's empowerment magazine with a team of women, called findyourbeautiful.com, which included articles written by top professionals in their respective fields. Michell and her partner hosted empowerment lifestyle events and workshops all over the province. Five years after the creation of her online magazine, Michell decided to take a break to, in her own words, perform the deepest heart surgery on herself. Now, she has decided to share this journey with other women through a different kind of medium, a book.

Michell has been through a wide array of experiences. From beginning Motherhood at the age of 17, growing up in a poor household which did not include a father, being in abusive relationships, to starting a business, and rising through the ranks to become the Vice President of Marketing for a well known real estate company, she has experienced a life of ups and downs, and now she wants to share it in the hopes it may help other women who are going through the same or similar issues.

Tools

Below are some tools which have helped and continue to help me in my journey of healing and awareness. I work on myself on a daily basis, so I want to share the resources in case you are in need of some to get you started on your wellness journey.

1. Podcasts: listen to podcasts all the time, specifically Elevation with Steve Furtick, Oprah's Super Soul Conversation, The School of Greatness, The Read, Trained by Nike, Rise with Rachel Hollis.
2. Books: The Four agreements, Love & Respect, Start with Why, Love Your Life, The Slight Edge and of course this one.
3. Meditation: They say all you need is to meditate for 15 minutes a day, so start with 5 minutes and build up to 15 minutes. There are also meditation videos which I sometimes listen to on YouTube before I fall asleep.
4. Surround yourself with good people who can bring more awareness into your life.
5. Music: listen to music which not only entertains you but inspires you.
6. Videos: The same as music, do not only watch videos which will entertain you, but watch documentaries and sermons or interviews.

Quotes

"Real integrity is doing the right thing, knowing that nobody's going to know whether you did it or not."
- Oprah Winfrey

"You can't make decisions based on fear and the possibility of what might happen." - Michell Obama

"Change will not come if we wait for some other person or some other time. We are the ones we've been waiting for. We are the change that we seek."
- Barack Obama

"Not everybody is perfect, and I don't think we should be looking for perfect people." - Simon Cowell

"Only God can judge me so I'm gone, either love me or leave me alone." - Jay z

"The most alluring thing a woman can have is confidence." - Beyonce

The right pair of shoes can change the feel of an outfit, and even change how a woman feels about herself."
- Fergie

"It's the messy parts that make us human, so we should embrace them too - pat ourselves on the back for getting through them rather than being angry for having gotten into them in the first place." -Jennifer Lopez

"If you put that effort in, you'll get what you want"- Kim Kardashian West

"I refuse to accept other people's ideas of happiness for me. As if there's a 'one size fits all' standard for happiness." - Kanye West

"I'm a real man. I can suffer." - Nicky Jam

"I'm selfish, impatient and a little insecure. I make mistakes, I am out of control and at times hard to handle. But if you can't handle me at my worst, then you sure as hell don't deserve me at my best." - Marilyn Monroe

"The universe that created you, and gave you all of your amazing talents, will support you in everything that you want." - Marisa Peer

"Too many people spend money they haven't earned, to buy things they don't want, to impress people they don't

like." - Will Smith

"Women, you can have it all - a loving man, devoted husband, loving children, a fabulous career."
- Jada Pinkett Smith

"If you want to change the direction of your life, change the declaration of your lips" - Steven Furtick

"My joy is not determined by what happens to me, but what Christ is doing in me and through me."
- Holly Furtick

"I think beautiful is like looking like you take care of yourself." - Cardi B

"Would you like me to give you a formula for success? It's quite simple, really: Double your rate of failure. You are thinking of failure as the enemy of success. But it isn't at all. You can be discouraged by failure or you can learn from it, so go ahead and make mistakes. Make all you can. Because remember that's where you will find success."– Thomas J. Watson

"I have insecurities of course, but I don't hang out with

anyone who points them out to me." - Adele

"To achieve anything great in life you must be willing to make a sacrifice." - Kelly Rowland

"Some people want it to happen, some wish it would happen, others make it happen." - Michael Jordan

"Everything negative - pressure, challenges - is all an opportunity for me to rise." - Kobe Bryant

"I'm a winner each and every time I go into the ring." - George Foreman

"I learned that courage was not the absence of fear, but the triumph over it." - Nelson Mandela

"If you're white and you're wrong, then you're wrong; if you're black and you're wrong, you're wrong. People are people. Black, blue, pink, green – God make no rules about color; only society make rules where my people suffer, and that why we must have redemption and redemption now." - Bob Marley

Have the courage to follow your heart and intuition. They somehow already know what you truly want to become. Everything else is secondary." - Steve Jobs

"We're running the company to serve more people." - Mark Zuckerberg

"Most men are fragile." - Taraji P. Henson

"We make the future sustainable when we invest in the poor, not when we insist on their suffering." - Bill Gates

"It's the mark of a backward society - or a society moving backward - when decisions are made for women by men." - Melinda Gates

"You are imperfect, you are wired for struggle, but you are worthy of love and belonging." - Brené Brown

"We delight in the beauty of the butterfly, but rarely admit the changes it has gone through to achieve that beauty." - Maya Angelou

977970 3339

97

Made in the USA
Middletown, DE
05 October 2021